Your Pocket Guide to a Career in Recruitment

By Stefan Stacey

Contents

Dedication

For Carys, with thanks for all your support, belief and patience.

Preface

Working in recruitment is an unpredictable and frivolous job. In my experience 70% of recruiters you meet are merely passing through and don't intend to pursue a career in this line of work. As a result, there's a severe lack of enthusiasm when it comes to training new team members, as it's often perceived that they won't be in the job for the long haul.

Prior to the economic downturn in 2008/9 every recruitment company I worked for, or interviewed with, had a very robust and thorough training program. Unfortunately, the training department was also one of the first departments to suffer as a result of the recession. UK recruitment businesses have since seemingly failed to recover from this rationalisation, and a lack of well-trained recruiters is now prevalent in the industry.

This is the main reason I have decided to publish a "training manual" in the form of the guide you now see in front of you.

In this guide I'm going to focus on permanent recruitment within the UK recruitment industry, with insights that are transferable to recruitment in any country. I will be covering recruitment as a whole, giving you the tools you need to become a successful recruitment consultant; one that stands out from the crowd, because the first thing you need to know is that "people buy from people".

Regardless of where you go, people are always looking for work, or need someone to do a job for them. The process of recruiting the right person is a time consuming and often-expensive process. Not only does the recruitment process detract from your daily job, (an often overlooked additional cost of recruitment), but the cost of getting it wrong can also far outweigh the cost of a good recruiter.

By the end of this guide you will have a good understanding of what you need to do in order to identify great candidates, and the juicy jobs likely to help you build a successful career as a recruiter.

Chapter 1: Introduction

Have you ever thought about a career in recruitment but weren't sure what was in store for you?

Maybe you've just started working as a recruitment consultant but found yourself in a company that doesn't have a set training programme, or perhaps you're keen to build on the training you've received and looking for more answers to your questions…

Maybe you're sitting on the fence about starting a career in recruitment and you're looking for a little more information on the role to help you decide.

If what you need is more information on recruitment, the recruitment process, the methods used in recruitment or the activities you need to do in order to become successful, then this guide will give you the basic tools you will need to see you through your first year in recruitment, and beyond.

This handy guide is for anyone either looking to start out in recruitment, or wanting to know more. It will cover recruitment in general, dealing with candidates and clients, filling jobs and understanding the processes you need to follow in order to become successful.

Recruitment can be a very lucrative industry, where successful recruitment consultants can easily earn over six figures per annum in some industries. With 5 years' experience, basic salaries can range from £35,000 upwards depending on the level you are recruiting at, with the opportunity to more than double that in bonuses throughout the year. This guide can help you tap into an industry where hard work really does reap rewards!

Chapter 2: People Buy from People

What is Recruitment?

In its most basic form, recruitment is the art of matching candidates to a client's needs. In its more advanced form; recruitment is a consultancy role that never rests.

In order to be a great recruiter you'll need to be knowledgeable of a number of areas:

- Market behaviour: the industries current and past market trends and future prospects

- Your client: you will have conducted in-depth research on them to understand their culture, operating processes, the benefits of joining the company as well as the pitfalls, their hierarchy and style of operation, who are the decision-makers and the potential stumbling blocks to your success.

- Your candidates: you will have met them all and are able to speak about their achievements with confidence and match them to potential clients, whilst keeping their career goals in mind.

- Talk with knowledge and confidence, and offer sound advice based on your past experience.

But where do you find these candidates or the clients you can place them with?

Before we get started, you must appreciate that in recruitment you will come across many people, both clients and candidates. Clients will become candidates, and your candidates will eventually become your clients. Because you are dealing with people every day, you will constantly be building relationships... and potentially burning some bridges along the way too. The art to successful recruitment is to retain and maintain the lucrative relationships you build exclusively.

Types of Recruiters

There are two types of recruiters: the *CV Sender* and the *Consultant*.

The CV sender

This recruitment style involves sending as many CV's to the client as possible, often known as *spaghetti flinging*. This is a volume-based business model where the recruiter will be working mainly off a company database that has thousands of candidates registered with their CV and details listed. You often find that the job details will be taken from the client over the phone, and the required skill set is entered into the database search parameters, which then produces a number of matches. These matches are then sent to the client for their role and if the client requests an interview with any of the candidates, only then are the candidates contacted to arrange interviews. The recruiter's time is mainly spent interviewing a vast amount of applicants from job adverts, populating their database and sending CV's to client accounts they are managing, and jobs they are working on. Not much time is spent developing relationships with prospective clients.

The Consultant

This is a more in-depth style of recruitment, where the recruiter will get to know the client and their culture and aims to forge long-term relationships. A full brief is taken for the role, often at a face-to-face meeting to assist the client in their brief, and to consult and manage their expectations. A full search is then conducted across the industry, in addition to their database, and a long list of suitable candidates is compiled. Face-to-face interviews are then conducted with each candidate, (or a call if they have already been met previously), to assess their current situation and suitability. This long list is then whittled down to 3 or 4 of the most suitable candidates based on the clients expectations and the brief. These candidates are then presented to the client with salary expectations and other relevant details over the phone or face-to-face. Management of the process, from start to finish, is imperative to guarantee success. This type of recruitment is typically referred to as *360-degree recruitment* because you will deal with all aspects of recruitment including candidates, clients and job roles.

There are two types of candidate: *active candidates* and *passive candidates.*

The Active Candidate

Active candidates, as the name suggests, are those candidates that are actively applying for jobs. They will be applying for roles directly and using agencies to assist them in their job search. Active candidates are easily found because they have an online presence and can often be found listed on some 3rd party databases. An active candidate may be interviewing with a number of different companies simultaneously so it is very important to keep track of where they have been, the companies they have interviewed with, the agencies that are representing them and what interviews they have coming up, lest you lose contact with them or they receive another job offer whilst you are representing them. According to a recent LinkedIn survey, active candidates only make up 30% of the workforce in the UK.

The Passive Candidate

Passive candidates are those candidates not currently applying for jobs. Many of them are happily employed but may be open to interesting or exciting career opportunities. As a result, many passive candidates are not on the radar of other recruiters. The majority of the UK workforce is made up of passive candidates and knowing how to find great passive candidates is a skill every great recruiter has to master.

Chapter 3: A Structured Approach

There are a number of methods used in recruitment in order to be successful; from managing large corporate accounts, through to targeted searching and headhunting. This chapter covers the most popular methods.

1. Account Management

The Account Management approach is a simple and easy-to-manage approach that utilizes one main point of contact for the client, and an ongoing focus on generating a high volume of candidate applications. With this approach you should ideally have a dedicated resourcer aiding and assisting you. You focus purely on a small number of clients, fully covering the candidate and job cycles, spending the majority of your time on the phone or in face-to-face interviews with candidates in order to assess their suitability for your clients. With this approach you are targeting a generalist position and fielding applications, or a similar position across all the client accounts you manage. The candidates applying could be a fit for a number of your businesses, or roles. This approach focuses fully on the candidate, generating a large amount of new applicants for you to meet and interview with the intention of filling your vacancies.

This approach is very useful for attracting active candidates. This approach also works well for a high volume recruitment business, such as one with a number of similar corporate accounts who typically have between 5 and 10 live vacancies each week.

2. Search & Selection

Search and selection is an ad hoc approach that utilises the full strength of your networks, database and advertising to find a suitable solution for your client. Vacancies are often picked up through daily business development, or as a result of following up leads. Having a selection of candidates at hand to send to the client whilst on the phone is advantageous. This is a multi-method approach to sourcing candidates, particularly advertising, as you will want to be meeting and interviewing as many as possible in order to build a large pool of potential candidates for a number of similar clients.

This method works well with contingency recruitment; one-off projects where a client has a specific need or vacancy to fill and you are required to search for and select the most appropriate candidates for interview.

3. Dedicated Search

Dedicated Search is a specialised and proactive approach involving heavy research. Also known as headhunting, this approach targets the right talent within the marketplace.

Using this approach you do more than just make contact with everyone on your database and other networks; after developing the brief with your client you begin to talent map the industry, identifying those specific individuals that meet the job's requirements, and then approach them on your client's behalf.

A dedicated search is often used when a client has very specific needs. This approach works well when focusing on the passive candidate.

4. Retained & Exclusive

This is more often than not the most profitable approach. The client has not only signed on with you and no one else (exclusivity), but they have also paid a small portion of your fee upfront (a retainer) to retain your services until the vacancy has been filled.

This is the more committed approach, as you are retained until you find a suitable candidate to fill the job. By utilizing a mix of Dedicated Search, and Search & Selection methodology you ensure you have taken all individuals into consideration, both active and passive candidates. By prioritizing this vacancy you ensure a timely and successful turnaround, from start to finish, ensuring the client is kept in the loop at each stage.

5. Project-based Recruitment

Being able to pick up a role from the very beginning once a need has been identified, and being able to consult on the project until it's completed will allow you to use all your resources to find the right people for the job. Depending on the level of staff required, this may include open days and assessment centres. For example; with a restaurant from the time the design has begun, throughout the construction process, refurbishment, and until the doors open.

This is mainly location based, and you will need to conduct localised headhunting and advertising to fill the role. Often a fixed price is quoted for the entire project in order to work on the assignment from beginning to end.

Project based recruitment is often done on an exclusive basis and can consume many resources given the time frames required to complete the project.

Chapter 4: Be Prepared

The Recruitment Process

Recruitment is divided into 3 cycles:

1. The Candidate Cycle

2. The Job Cycle

3. The Client Cycle

Full 360-degree recruitment involves all 3 cycles. By mastering all 3 cycles you will be able to achieve that perfect synergy resulting in consistent success.

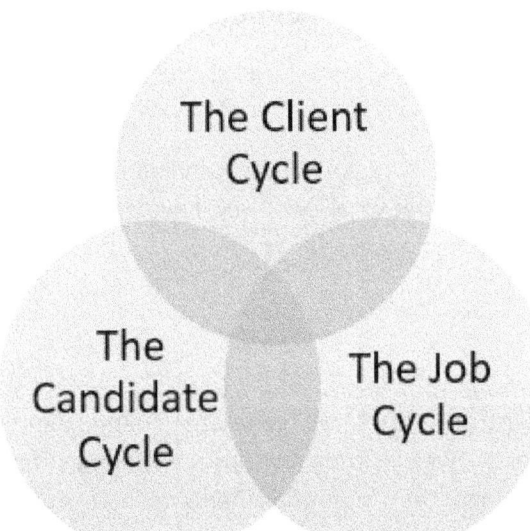

The Client Cycle

The Candidate Cycle

The Job Cycle

Junior consultants should start with the candidate cycle until mastered, then move onto the job cycle and finally finish with the client cycle. A typical timeframe would see a junior consultant spend at least 6 months purely on one cycle before moving on to take control of the next, ideally being able to do the full 3 cycles and targeting new business for development after all 3 are mastered, without the need for support. This would see the consultant rise from a junior consultant to a consultant after a year and before speaking to clients and developing business, to finally achieving senior consultant status after hitting all financial targets laid out for them 6-12 months after completing all 3 cycles.

Chapter 5: Product is Everything

The Candidate Cycle

This cycle deals purely with the candidate. Picking up in chronological order from once you have advertised a role and received responses.

1. Identifying the right candidate

A well-written advert will generate a large amount of response. A well-written CV speaks volumes about a candidate and their potential. Being able to quickly sift through 50 applications and identify potential candidates is a skill a good recruiter needs to hone and perfect. The average trained recruiter spends around 15 seconds looking at a CV. The decision you need to make is: "Is this person worth talking to in order to find out more about how good they are?"

Taking the client's criteria and the job description into account, the main areas to focus on are:

- The candidate's skill-set and abilities

- The candidate's capabilities e.g. volumes and turnovers, the number of staff they've managed, the size and number of sites they have managed

- The candidate's length of service

- The candidate's career progression

- The candidate's achievements in each role

All these areas will give you an idea of what they are capable of and their staying power.

Inevitably you will come across job hoppers; someone who changes jobs every year or two will be difficult to sell into a client in terms of their return on investment (ROI). There are exceptions however, such as chefs, who move around to different establishments annually in order to improve their skill-set. But on the whole, longevity and progression is important in any career.

When skimming through CV's, a good recruiter will firstly focus on the applicant's career history; the dates and length of service in each company they have worked and the names of the companies themselves. Having a stable career history, and one or two of the industry leaders in the market will be looked on more favourably than not. Career progression and the candidate's achievements come next.

Set aside some time every morning to go through all your applications and call every worthwhile candidate. Follow up your call with a voicemail, a text message and an email if you are unable to reach them. If you succeed in getting in touch with them, then proceed onto the telephone interview.

2. The Telephone Interview

If they are good enough to call, are they good enough to meet? The idea behind a telephone interview is to ascertain whether or not the candidate fits your job criteria and parameters, and if they are worth meeting face-to-face for any potential roles you may have coming up, deal with generally, or already have on your books.

It is always a good idea to work off a question sheet and fill out the answers given. This way you can update their CV with the detail they have provided and cross-reference any information they give you if they come in to meet you, or use the information for other purposes such as business development (BD) or research.

TIP: Always have an objective before you pick up the phone – "What do I want to get out of this call?"

Your questions should be focused with a potential job or company in mind. The main question you should be asking yourself is: "Is this person worth bringing in to spend an hour with?" A telephone interview should last no longer than 20 minutes.

Your telephone interview should cover the following areas:

- Candidate Name & Address

- Salary - current and expected

- Location and parameters i.e. how far will they travel

- Notice Period

- Reasons for leaving

- Position and responsibilities

- Job specific capabilities

- Roles applied for and agencies they are working with, have already registered with or met

- Right to work in UK

Upon beginning the call you should always introduce yourself and the business you work for, stating the reason for your call and asking them if they are free to talk at present.

Confirm their personal details and needs/wants and then work through their career history starting with the most recent job, working back chronologically. You need only cover 5 years or 3 job roles that are relevant; the rest can be done when you meet face-to-face.

What do they sound like over the phone? Are they confident or do they need to think a lot before giving you answers? If you feel that they are worth meeting, then invite them in for a face-to-face.

TIP: Take into account that a candidate may not be in an ideal place or situation to discuss their job search when you call. Always ask them if they are free to talk or able to speak freely.

A candidate who has already registered with several agencies or has applied to several companies directly is going to be difficult to manage and possibly not worth representing, unless you have one specific job for which they have not previously applied.

Once you have agreed on a time and date to meet the candidate, send them an email to confirm your meeting and add it to your diary. Along with the email include the need for them to bring their passport or relevant documents in order to prove their right to work in the UK. Placing candidates that have no legal right to work in the UK can carry fines of up to £20,000 per candidate in the UK (known as a civil penalty).

3. The Face-to-Face Interview

A face-to-face interview is the ideal opportunity to assess a candidate's performance, as they would perform at interview for one of your clients. This is a consultative process so be prepared to provide feedback afterward.

Before they arrive

As Lord Baden Powell famously said: "Be Prepared!" At no other stage in the candidate cycle is this quote more important.

Prior to your candidate arriving you should have their CV printed out along with previous notes you made during your telephone interview. You should have an idea of the areas you want to cover in the interview, and the jobs you would like to discuss with the candidate. If you believe the candidate is good enough for one of your colleagues roles then ensure they too are aware the candidate is coming in and you would like them to meet as well (providing they are suitable).

A face-to-face interview should last for around an hour. In order to cover everything you should follow a structured interview style.

The interview

Upon arrival the candidate should be given a registration form to complete often done by you, your receptionist or the person who has let them in through the door. This form will ask for their personal details, reference material or reference contact details and confirm that they have brought their ID with them or some other form of proof that they are legally entitled to work in the UK. This is in order to ensure your business is adhering to the laws on compliance and standard practices in the UK for recruitment businesses. The registration form should also include any other agencies they are registered with and any jobs they have applied to in the last 12 months. In the UK, it is standard practise for an agency to claim ownership of a candidate for 12 months after submitting their CV to a client. You do not want to send a candidates CV to the same client within this time and risk having another agency claim the fee for your hard work.

Once they have completed this, you can then take them to the interview area.

A. The greeting and introduction

If you've not already done so, greet the candidate and ask how they are, how their journey was or their day thus far; you will find out more from a relaxed person rather than someone nervous, so try to "break the ice". Introduce yourself and thank them for attending the meeting. Give them a brief explanation about the areas you intend to cover and the length of time it will take. Ask if they have any other appointments booked or if they need to return to work; anything which may cut the interview short and will result in you having to adjust your interview so that they can leave with enough time to get to their next appointment.

B. Personal Details

Confirm their personal details from the registration form; address, telephone, email etc. Ensure you cover the best ways to contact them.

"What is the best way to get in touch with you?"

"Would you mind if I text you if you don't answer the phone?"

"How often do you check email?"

"How much notice do you need for interview?'

Ask them what they have done thus far to find a job. Knowing how long they've been applying for jobs, the agencies they are currently working with, and their interview success since their job search began is very telling and important to your success as a recruiter. Unless you are interviewing them for a specific role, a candidate that has been looking for work for more than 3 months, has already applied to a number of companies including some of the market leaders in your industry and is registered with 3 or more other agencies, is going to be very difficult to place.

C. The CV and Career History

Start by offering some advice on their CV, its content and length. If your company has a standard format they use when presenting a CV then explain to the candidate the changes you will make. When covering their career history, begin with their most recent job first and work back chronologically. If you have conducted a thorough telephone interview you will already have covered the basics of their responsibilities, financials and skills, and you should now be looking to cover their achievements for each role and gather company information for your own future Business Development or referencing. If you haven't done a thorough telephone interview then you must cover these details now. Understanding a candidate's achievements is very important. Not only will it give you an insight into how the candidate operates and the skills they have developed, but also assist you in selling the candidate to the client by highlighting their achievements and how they accomplished them when talking about them. Aim to receive tangible results for every achievement, such as percentage increases to sales each year or quarter, the number of new staff members trained and developed, exact numbers when it comes to cost savings etc.; everything a potential employer will find attractive.

D. Competency Interview Questions

Competency questions are designed to test a candidate's performance under certain situations and/or their behaviours. With proper competency training you will be able to devise questions based on your client's job description and requirements. If you have invited your candidate to interview with a specific job in mind, then ensure you have prepared a few competency questions based on the job description and specifics the client is looking for.

Most common competencies begin with: "Tell me about a time when..." or "Describe a situation where..." The perfect answer a candidate can give to competency question should begin with a clear description of the situation or background, followed by the actions taken, (ensuring that the actions are personal to the candidate), and finished with the outcome or result, ideally positive. If the outcome was not positive ask the candidate how they dealt with this to get a positive outcome.

Well-answered competency questions will reinforce your reasons why the candidate is an ideal fit for the role you have shortlisted them. They can also form the basis of your sales pitch to clients or any other vacancy you may represent them for.

E. Personality

Following competency questioning you will want to understand your candidate's personality, their strengths and weaknesses, development needs, and possibly their management style and career aspirations. Ask the candidate directly for each of these and note down their answers. Some of the answers you receive will assist in creating your introduction of the candidate to your clients.

F. What the candidate wants

Having thoroughly covered their behaviours, it is time to cover the candidate's needs/wants, locations they will consider working in, their salary expectations and counter offers, and their motivation for moving jobs. This is one of the most important stages in the face-to-face interview, as it will allow you to test the candidate's commitment and give you an understanding of what they really want. This will also help you predict which offers they are likely to take and increase your success as a recruiter.

Questions to ask include:

- What are you looking for in your next role?

- What 3 things will motivate you in your next job?

- Of the 3 you mentioned, if you could only have 2, which would you choose?

G. Feedback

Give them brief, honest and positive feedback on their interview technique including body language and how to answer questions, and then move onto the jobs you have in mind for them.

H. Jobs

Having interviewed the candidate you should have a good understanding which of your clients cultures they will fit into, the roles that they can do and which companies they will suit. Cover live jobs you would like to send them to as well as speculative companies you would like to represent them to. Tell them that you will email them these options so that they can research the businesses and get back to you with feedback.

I. Compliance and References

If you haven't already received it, make a copy of their passport as mentioned earlier, or some form of ID to confirm their details and that they are legally allowed to work in the UK. Double-check their reference details. If they have supplied any references from a current employer you must ask them when they are happy for you to contact that particular reference, particularly if the candidate has not yet handed in notice. Phoning their current employer who is unaware that the candidate is leaving could lead to negative repercussions for both the candidate and yourself.

Any written references must be filed and used when required, either attached to the CV to support the candidate's application or along with their acceptance of a job offer. In line with UK law, verbal references should only be checked at final interview stage or upon receipt of a job offer. Be sure to receive the details of the candidate's line manager instead of the contact details for the Human Resources department, as this will get a more personal reference. Many companies will prefer to check references themselves, so ensure you provide them with the correct contact details and ask the candidate to confirm that the referee is aware of their obligation.

J. Meeting the team

Always try and introduce the candidate to another consultant, especially if you are unsure about the candidate in some way or need a colleague to give their opinion. Your colleagues may also have suitable jobs for your candidate. Introduce them and either say good-bye to the candidate and give them your card, or ensure you will see them to the door once your colleagues are finished meeting the candidate.

After the Interview

A. Follow up

Probably the most important part of the candidate cycle is the follow up. Email the candidate and thank them for their time as well as including the companies and roles you have discussed and will be representing them to. Ask them to confirm by replying that they agree for you to represent them. Not only is this a legal prerequisite when acting as an agent, but also, should another agency represent the same candidate to the same client and there is a dispute over ownership of the candidate, you will have written confirmation and proof that the candidate has given you their express permission to act on their behalf when dealing with the client in question. This will also confirm the dates your meeting took place should a client claim that they received the candidate's application directly or found them online. Should the dispute go to court, you will need written evidence to back up your claim.

B. CV and Notes

Once the candidate has left it is time to gather all your notes and format their CV, add any additional information from both the phone and face-to-face interviews to the CV, and create a cover sheet for the candidate.

A cover sheet should be 3 or 4 sentences introducing the candidate to the client before they open the CV. It should include a brief description of the candidate and their personality, management style, work ethic or cultural fit that matches what the client requires. You should also include 2 competencies or achievements from your interview that the client will find advantageous; reasons they are suitable for the role. Finally, it must include the candidate's notice period and salary expectations for the role.

C. The Candidate Registration Pack

Ideally the candidate's CV, passport or ID copy, references and interview notes from both the telephone and face-to-face interview should be kept together and then filed. A candidate pack must be held for future reference and all documents filed away. This must be retained for at least 6 months or as long as you are still representing the candidate and should be kept up-to-date during this time.

In the UK, any individual has a legal right to access all data that is kept on them, including the notes made from your interviews. You must ensure this data is housed securely. Out-of-date data can carry legal implications and a hefty fine should you be found to be in breach of the UK Data Protection Act. Data of any candidate that you are not currently representing or have not spoken to within 12 months must be disposed of securely. Ensure you dispose of the data safely and in accordance with current legislation.

4. Other points to consider

A. Halos vs. Horns

Many inexperienced recruiters fall into the trap, where they meet a candidate and are instantly either put off by them or feel that they are *gold-dust* but unable to back up either claim. A thorough and practical recruiter will be able to disregard either of these, and gauge a candidate on their place-ability. If the candidate fits the clients' profile and requirements and answers all your competencies correctly, then they should be put forward as suitable. If you are still unsure of the candidate's suitability then try asking some of your colleagues for their opinion and follow up on the allowed references given to you by the candidate. Your final option is to call the client and speak through the candidate's CV and background with them, and why they would be suitable. If the client is interested they will ask you for their availability for interview.

B. Open vs. Closed Questions

A closed question is one with a YES or NO answer. Asking who, what, where, how and why are open questions, and these will ensure that the candidate talks at length. All questions asked should be open questions unless you only want a confirmation. When conducting an interview with a candidate you should aim to do no more than 30% of the talking, therefore open questions are advisable.

C. Reigning Them In

Some candidates have a tendency to talk a lot and often venture off-topic. If this happens, stop them and either ask them the question again but in a different way, or move onto the next question. A simple: "I'm sorry but we are moving off topic" or "Let me just stop you there quickly..." will often work well.

D. Their Career

As a career recruiter you will find that your candidates will eventually become your clients. Taking care of their career and treating them as future clients from the beginning of your relationship is one of the more important things to bear in mind.

Remember: People will buy from people – creating a good impression will set you apart from any of your competitors.

Most recruiters will have a long list of jobs to fill and will try and push every candidate that they meet into the roles they are currently working on, even if those roles don't suit the candidate. Constantly having to deal with candidates leaving the job prematurely, with rebates, or with free replacements, are signs that you have not done your job as *The Consultant* but rather have acted as *The CV Sender*. It is also a sure sign that you have not listened to the candidate or asked the right questions when discussing their career and aspirations.

E. Spoon-feeding & Coaching

A successful recruiter pulls out all the stops in order to ensure their candidates are successful at interview. Part of getting to know your client is to do your research, to meet with them and conduct visits to their sites. An organised recruiter will type up their client notes for future reference and a good recruiter will share this information with their candidates. Giving your candidate the best chance to get the job will ensure you are that much more successful, even if it means aiding them with all their research.

Chapter 6: Process Driven Activities

The Job Cycle

Often new consultants will begin their careers as a Resourcer mastering the Candidate Cycle of recruitment first, followed by the Job Cycle and then the Client Cycle. However, Resourcers will also conduct the majority of advertising and candidate searching whilst working at this level. In this chapter I will chronologically cover all the stages of the Job Cycle, from picking up the job, through to advertising, sourcing and placement.

Once picked up, the life cycle of a job consists of 5 phases; namely The Job Details, Resourcing, Shortlisting, The Interview Process and Offer Acceptance. A recruiter's job doesn't end there however, as you will still need to manage the candidate until they have not only started their job, but also passed their probation period. A candidate that doesn't start or leaves before they pass probation will often result in a credit to the client or you may be forced to re-recruit the role for a replacement. Be sure to check your companies guarantee policy on rebates for these details.

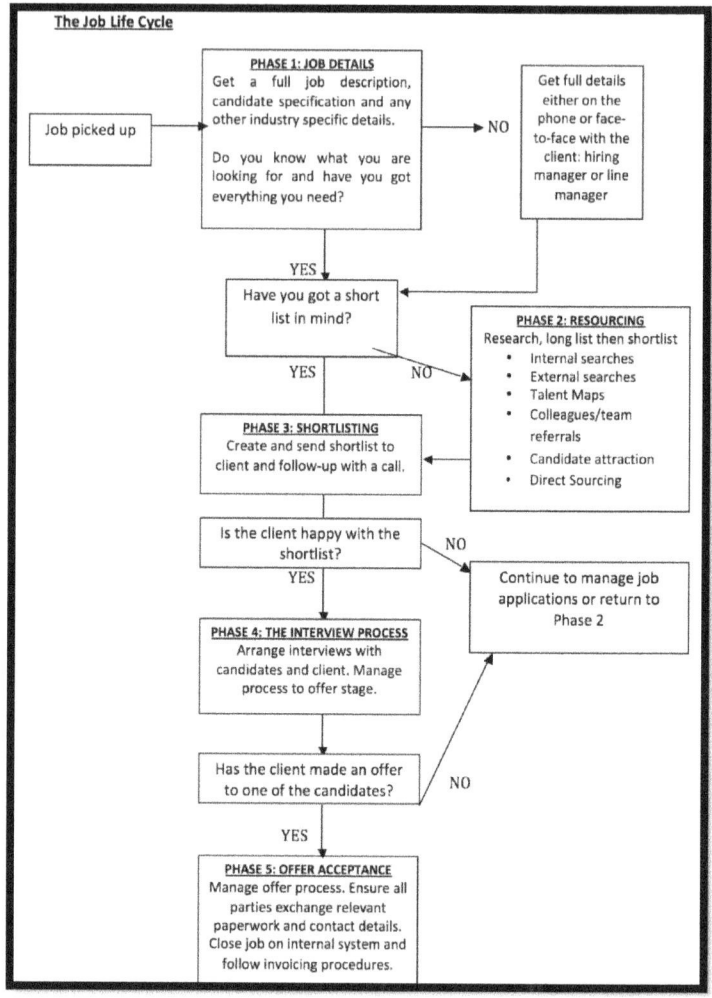

Picking up the Job

Arrange a client meeting for all new clients and for any jobs where an existing client cannot provide you with a job description, where you are unable to get all the information you need over the phone, or where you have not recruited this type of role for your client before. There are a number of ways to go about picking up a new job:

A. Managed Accounts

The easiest way to receive jobs is by having a number of accounts where you are listed as a preferred supplier on the clients PSL (preferred supplier list), particularly for corporate accounts. These can often bring in 5-10 jobs every week due to the high demand for staff the client has.

B: Advertising

You have seen a job advertised. After some research you ring up the client and ask to work on the role. You may already have the perfect candidate available, based on their job description and candidate specification, and, because you have met and interviewed them in depth, you are easily able to discuss the candidate and the reasons for their suitability for this particular role. This is called a speculative sale. If done correctly, a good recruiter will also be able to arrange initial interviews for the candidate whilst still on the phone without the need for sending a CV. Thereafter you can call your candidate to inform them that you have secured them an interview should they decide they would like to go forward. Once agreed you then send the client confirmation of the interview along with the candidate's CV and your company Terms of Business if you haven't already discussed them over the phone. With practice you will be able to perform this type of speculative introduction flawlessly.

C. Business Development

Throughout the course of your career in recruitment, it can often happen that you call one of your target clients asking them if there are any vacancies that you can assist them with and they say yes. Business development is covered in more depth under the Client Cycle.

D. Referral/Recommendation

Clients will often call in jobs; sometimes as a result of you being referred by someone you have done business with in the past. Many of these jobs will come to you exclusively either as the client's first option, or because they have a vacancy they haven't had success filling either on their own, or with other agencies.

E. Social Media

Similar to advertising where you spot jobs being advertised or discussed through Twitter, Facebook, LinkedIn etc.

Phase 1: Job Details

A. The Job Description

In order to have the best chance of success in filling your job you need to ensure you have all the details to hand from the client. Never work on a job with only half the information required, otherwise you are setting yourself up to fail. As someone starting out in recruitment, always remember: the more you know, the more successful you will be.

If the client is unable to provide a full job description you will have to create your own. Either use a company provided template, or you can use the one provided here. You will require the following:

- The job title and salary on offer
- When the client needs the role filled by (immediately/2 months etc.)
- How urgent is the job
- Who else is working on the role
- Who does the role report into
- Who supports this role and what support is available
- What staff responsibilities are there; direct reports, departments etc.
- What are the responsibilities and scope of the role
- What skills, experience and competencies are required for the role

- Why has the job arisen

B. Package Details

Confirm the salary and benefits package, the details of the bonus (if any), holiday allowance, car or living expenses, healthcare, pension etc.

C. The Ideal Candidate

Ask the client to describe their ideal candidate and what they are looking for in a person. Understand the cultural fit and personality of the ideal candidate. Questions to consider asking include:

- What experience or background is necessary to be successful in this position

- What is the background of the person leaving the position

- What is the best culture fit and the team dynamic

- What 3 things would stand out on a CV for you

D. Interview Process

Gather all the information on the interview process as well as any dates they have already put aside for interviews. Including the following:

- How many stages are there

- Who will be present at each stage

- What structure will each interview take

- Will the candidate be required to do a presentation or business plan

- What is the timescale from receiving a shortlist to interview and finally to offer

- How many CV's do you expect to receive

- How do you expect candidates to be presented at each stage

- Who are the points of contact during the recruitment process

E. Closing

At this stage, if you have not already done so, you should send your fees to the client to be agreed, or book in a client meeting to discuss them face-to-face. Pre-existing fees should already be stored on file. Fees are dealt with in more detail under the Client Cycle. Once timescales and expectations have been agreed you can move on to the next phase and begin resourcing your job.

If it is your first time recruiting for your client and you are unsure of what they are looking for but want to test your understanding, it is acceptable practice to send the client a preliminary shortlist of 3 candidates (while still on the phone) and ask for the client's feedback. This shortlist must include one candidate that meets all their requirements on target, especially salary, one candidate that is overqualified and asking for 10-20% more remuneration over target, and one candidate that can do the job and is either inexperienced or requires some initial support, but is asking for around 20% less remuneration under target. These candidates should be ones that either you or your colleagues have met and dealt with before, and come highly regarded. This may give you a better indication of what the client is looking for whilst reassuring the client that you have a number of good candidates already registered with your agency.

Phase 2: Resourcing

The next phase in the job life cycle focuses on the candidate and attracting the right applicants to your job through various candidate attraction methods. Every good recruiter will already know a number of suitable candidates off the top of their head. Jot these names down as the beginning of your long list.

Filling a role is a systematic process starting with internal/in-house candidates and then covering external candidates, both active and passive.

Once you have picked up a job, in addition to any candidates that immediately spring to mind, begin resourcing by running searches on your company database and refer to your own lists of readily available candidates and previous shortlists for similar jobs. Refer to any talent mapping or industry mapping you may have done.

Next, share the job internally by speaking to your team and colleagues, asking them for any candidates that cross their minds or any recommendations they may have.

Search any 3rd party databases and websites you have access to, including LinkedIn. Run searches on job boards and refer to any alerts you may already have set up.

Begin external candidate attraction including advertising, social media and direct sourcing.

A: Advertising & Social Media

The art of attracting the right candidates to your job can be done through the use of social media and advertising, referrals and recommendations and good old-fashioned headhunting.

Follow a structured approach to creating your advert. Make use of headers, hooks (attractive features of the job and company) and clear, concise language to attract the candidates you want.

There are a number of basic pieces of information, which need to be included in your advert. Begin by listing the job title, then the salary and benefits on offer, the work location and the sector the job is working in. Listed under separate headers should be information on the company if the company is being publicly advertised, the role and the candidate you are looking for. Finish the advert with ways to apply.

A well-written advert should not only have a good response rate, but should attract the right calibre of candidate you are looking for too. Then use your preferred methods of social media, Twitter or LinkedIn, to market your job.

You should set aside some time every morning to check your advert response and reply accordingly. Contact suitable candidates and offer regrets to those who are not suitable. Adverts attract mainly active candidates who will be interviewing for a number of roles simultaneously, so you cannot afford to waste time lest they get an offer before you have found time to call them.

Once you have a hardy database of great candidates, advertising should really only be used as a tool to generate more candidates to top up your database, or replace the active ones you have placed.

B. Headhunting/Direct Sourcing

If done correctly this is probably the cheapest and most effective way of directly sourcing candidates. Headhunting done properly will require a lot of your time and focus. Headhunting should be done discreetly either over the phone or in person. Exercise care when finding candidates with this method, pay particular attention to your supplier agreement and any non-poaching clauses.

When you get to speak to your target audience, you need to deal with them in an upfront and flattering manner. Don't give too much away until you get their buy-in and CV, otherwise they may apply directly to your client and you will lose out on a fee.

A conversation could go something like this:

"Hello, I'm looking for the manager on Duty from last week Friday..." or *"Hello, I'm calling from a national headhunting firm. My researcher / team was in the area along with our client (last Friday) and identified you/your business as a potential fit for the role they have currently retained us for. In fact, my researcher was very excited when he/she was telling me about you."*

"Now I know you are at work at the moment and it's not easy to talk, but I would like to send you some background information on ourselves, to show you that are a professional company, as well as a link to my profile so you are comfortable with the fact that I do this regularly."

"What time do you finish work today so I can call you?"

"Great, what is the best number to contact you on after working hours? What is your email address so I can send you my details?"

Candidate: Can I have the name of the client?

"Yes, of Course... why don't you give me your number and I will call you after your shift today to discuss them. In the meantime I can email you some details about my background and the company I am calling from..."

Follow up for CV:

"Hi... we spoke earlier/yesterday about the opportunity I have at the moment. As you can imagine I don't know much about your background and would prefer to receive a current CV from you (whatever you have on file) so my client can get a better understanding of your experience. Clearly my client has taken an interest in you and likes the way you operate but I need to be able to discuss this with them (which of course I don't have). When do you think you can send it to me?"

On occasion your client may have already identified the companies and backgrounds you should target, and the level of experience you are looking for, or the location you should be focusing on.

If you are targeting competitors then you need to identify the businesses your ideal candidate will come from. If you are looking at a specific location then you should map out the catchment area and list the suitable businesses in that area.

Once identified you need to ring the sites to start name-gathering. Be discreet when calling places of work – you wouldn't want to speak to the boss and inadvertently let them know that their staff are being headhunted. I have found that being direct and just asking for a name outright works well, or mention you want to leave feedback addressed directly to the site GM and ask for their details.

Once your name-gathering is completed then it is time to contact your targets to gauge their interest and request that they send a copy of their CV to you. Some candidates will be uninterested, others will be pushy and want to know the client name, and some of them will have a sense of grandeur fuelled by the ego boost that being headhunted brings with it. Throughout the conversation you need to remain calm and not give too much away until you have their CV in front of you. You still need to give them enough information to keep them interested and get them to send you their CV immediately.

Once you have their CV, conduct a telephone interview and collect all the relevant information you need to complete the CV. Send the candidate some company information or an assignment brief and ask them to do their research. Don't allow the candidate to become complacent just because they've been headhunted.

"Although the client has identified you as someone of interest, you still have to go through the HR process and impress the rest of the board in order to tick all their boxes. Obviously I am here to help with that…"

C. Talent Mapping (Proactive Direct Sourcing)

Talent mapping or proactive direct sourcing is something you should do on a regular basis - visiting your clients' competitors either on site or at industry events, with business card in hand, taking note of and approaching any potential candidates you meet.

An approach could go something like this:

"Wow, you really impressed me today with (the way you ran service). I'd like to give you my business card – if you are ever looking or just feel like putting your feelers out into the job market I would be delighted to represent you"

This is a non-intrusive approach and works very well when dealing with passive candidates.

D: Referrals & Recommendations

Your candidates are the best source for referrals and recommendations. When asking them about a role, if they are negative or don't sound interested, it is always a good idea to ask if they can recommend anyone or they know of anyone who may be interested in such an opportunity.

"Hello John, I'm currently recruiting for an Operations Director for a multinational company. The role includes overseeing 250 staff over 3 regions with another due to open. They are willing to pay up to £80,000 plus an achievable £20,000 bonus, car or travel allowance, pension and healthcare… Do you know of anyone who may be interested in such an opportunity?"

Nine times out of ten the candidate you are speaking to will either say yes they are interested, or they will give you a name of someone who could be interested.

A long list is the combined list of candidates you have in mind for the job, those you have sourced and those who have applied. A shortlist is your whittled down list of applicants post-vetting, who are the best candidates and are going to be submitted to the client.

When dealing exclusively on an assignment it is commonplace to update the client every second or third day in order to keep them up to speed with your progress. In the initial stages of working on the assignment the client will be interested in the candidates you are meeting and interviewing. Sending your longlist is a good way to update your client. This document can be continuously updated and worked off of during the assignments life cycle. More importantly, it can also be used to introduce and identify candidates to the client prior to meeting with them as well as asking the client to populate any additional candidates they think are worthwhile talking to.

The long list is an important document, which will not only aid you in showing the client the amount of work that has taken place, but it can also be used as an aid in getting paid if a candidate has been hired externally or through another agency but exists on the long list which the client has been provided with. This proves you identified the candidate to the client, and acts as an introduction, which is billable on many recruitment businesses terms and conditions.

The shortlist should always be sent to the client when working on a job, as these are the final candidates you are submitting for the role. Shortlists will generally include 3-5 CV's of the most suitable candidates, unless the client has stated they want to see more. Be very wary of this request as it often means that they client either doesn't trust your judgement, is unsure of what they are looking for, or they are not 100% committed to the process. You may end up re-recruiting this job or being led astray by a client that may just be testing the waters.

If you are an Account Manager with a list of jobs you will be constantly sending your client a stream of candidates you have met, vetted and matched according to their criteria. There is no need for shortlisting, because Account Management is an ongoing process. For all other recruitment methods it is commonplace to send the client a formal shortlist within the agreed timeframe with a précis for each candidate - reasons for each candidate's representation.

TIP: *Always follow up the sending of your shortlist with a call to discuss the candidates and to and arrange interviews.*

Phase 4: The Interview Process

Being able to co-ordinate the diaries of both candidates and your client can sometimes be tricky. Most candidates may only have one day a week when they are able to interview or only at a specific time during the day. Your client may want to act fast on the assignment or see everyone on one day or perhaps at one time every day for a week. Try and ensure a pre-emptive attitude to arranging interviews, always ensure you have backup options for both parties in the event one can't make the prearranged time.

Ensure your candidate is fully prepared and confirm the details in writing, (by email), with both parties. The more information, the better prepared. Don't be afraid to spoon-feed candidates. Most of them will appreciate it!

Ensure you include details such as

- Location & address with a link to Google maps

- Time and expected duration

- Interviewers

- Dress code

- Website links

- Hints and tips

- Job description, details and any supporting documentation

After each interview you should call your candidate for their feedback. It is important to know what they discussed, how they felt the interview went and any questions the candidate may have struggled on. Not only will this help in briefing other candidates, but also, when speaking to the client you will already know of the areas the candidate feels they could have done better in, discussing them with the client prior to them being brought up.

After all the feedback has been taken, liaise with the client to invite successful applicants to the next stage, arranging interviews, and rejecting the candidates that have not progressed to the next stage.

No doubt every candidate you represent is place-able, so ensure you give them clear reasons as to why they didn't progress, offering some pointers for the next time they interview, and any other relevant jobs or clients they may be interested in. Keep them positive and they will stay loyal to you.

Phase 5: Offer Acceptance

The most crucial part for any consultant is being able to close a deal. Through thorough interview techniques and direct questions of your candidate after each stage you should be able to predict whether or not they will accept the role you have put them forward for, and at what price. It is essentially up to you to get the offer you know the candidate will not only accept, but also where they will be happy to start in the role as soon as possible.

If you do encounter difficulties, the best way to counter this is to read back to the candidate the notes on their wants and motivations from their initial interview with you and match them against what they are being offered.

"When you came in to see me you said that you were looking for progression, an established company and a salary that at least matches what you are currently earning; in that order. I've managed to secure a role for you with progression to Area Manager after 12 months, provided you hit all targets set for you. It is working for (Company X), which is an international company with a good reputation for taking care of their staff and ensuring you get the progression and training you stated you were looking for. I have also managed to secure you a salary of £38,000 that matches what you are currently on, but additionally, you also have a 50% bonus potential that is target-based and very achievable."

The same can be said for the client. When working on Exclusive or Retained Assignments it is always beneficial to get the client to sign off the job details as picked up and discussed, in the event that they pull the assignment and go elsewhere, or cancel. An assignment that has been signed off and agreed, where you have done everything asked of you and ticked all the clients boxes in terms of candidates provided, is still chargeable as work successfully done, because there will usually be a clause in your terms stating this.

"When we met you stated that you were looking for XYZ. We discussed the details of the assignment and agreed on the parameters and terms, which you signed."

A. The Offer

When the client is prepared to make an offer, ensure that they email it to you so you can send it to your candidate, but also file it on your system. Get verbal and written acceptance from your candidate. If the candidate accepts, ensure that you confirm their contact details and their earliest start date for contractual purposes. Send these to your client along with any references or reference contacts informing the client of your invoicing procedures. Inform your candidate to hand in their notice once they have received, signed and returned their new contract of employment. Be sure to let your client know this so that they send the candidates contract out in a timely manner in order to ensure a faster turn-around.

B. Bedding in

Many recruitment companies will have a 3-month rebate/guarantee period from the date the candidate starts their new job. It is in your best interests to remain in touch with your newly placed candidate throughout their notice and probation period. You should put in a call every fortnight until their first month in the job, followed by a monthly call until they pass probation. Great candidates should always receive a call from you every 3-6 months thereafter in case their situation changes, they may be looking again or they may have been promoted. You never know; they may be in a position to hire staff themselves and you have then converted a candidate into a client.

Chapter 7: The Source of all our Income

The Client Cycle

This is the last and the most delicate cycle to master for any budding recruitment consultant looking to work across all 3 cycles in the recruitment process. It deals purely with the client, from finding potential clients, through to developing them, and converting them into current clients.

As clients are the source of all our income, only recruiters that are aware of their company's operating procedures and unique selling points should be making initial contact and sales calls. These recruiters are after all the voice of the company that they work for when it comes to marketing the business and the brand. A poorly prepared sales call to any potential client can not only tarnish your reputation with the client as a recruiter, but will also look bad for the company you work for. Repairing a damaged reputation takes time and patience and can sometimes lead to decreases in revenue in order to win back the client. Experienced recruiters should handle all sales calls to clients.

As a recruitment consultant developing new business, you must be able to confidently and flawlessly sell yourself, your business and the benefits received when using you to any potential client.

Whether you are starting a new desk, or picking up an existing desk, you will always be involved in business development. Business development is an ongoing process and can take various forms, from speaking to clients on the phone about candidates or current affairs, to visiting them on site or after hours for a catch up.

With client's where there is already a relationship, these activities are referred to as *relationship-building activities*. For any potential clients where we are hoping to win business and begin a relationship, we refer to these activities as *new business development*.

In order to be successful as a recruitment consultant you will need to have the ability to generate and manage your own list of clients that will eventually come directly to you when they have a recruitment need, instead of you going to them. New business development is an ongoing process and you must always be on the lookout for new clients to add to your list of potentials.

Identifying Potential Clients

If you have joined a large recruiting firm or organisation, chances are many of the well-known clients will already be active clients with your colleagues. A database of clients will already exist, listing which consultants in the business are responsible for each client. Ensure you exclude these clients from your business development plans to avoid duplication. Start by printing out a list of the clients that you have free reign to contact and begin targeting those clients with a telephone call to introduce yourself as the new contact for their account and ask if there are any roles you can assist them with. Because these clients have had contact from your company in the past, all of your calls will be to *warm contacts*.

If you have joined a business with a limited database, or you are starting a new desk from scratch, then you will need to begin by doing some industry research. Use the Internet, business directories and any related industry media to start mapping the relevant clients that you can target.

Through market mapping and research you can work out who and where the big spenders are and who has a high staff turnover. It is beneficial to have a mixed client list – a handful of big spenders you can Account Manage, and many small and medium sized operators who will come to you exclusively. This way you can spread your income across the sector and give candidates the option of various clients.

Next, categorise your potential clients into categories of A, B or C, depending on the amount of jobs they are likely to be recruiting; A being 1 or more jobs every week, B being 2 or more jobs every 3 months and C being 1 or 2 jobs a year. The frequency of your calls to each client should be proportional to the amount of jobs they recruit. Clients falling into the C category should only receive a call every 3-6 months, whilst your A-listed clients should be contacted weekly/fortnightly.

TIP: Don't try to work with every market leader. Many clients you come across will favour staff from their direct competitors. Working with every client in your sector will hinder your headhunting grounds, thereby limiting the potential candidates you can target.

Research

Probably the most important stage when contacting a client is to first do your research on them. You'll want to be knowledgeable about them, understand their product, culture, the staff fit, volumes and turnovers so you can understand what they are looking for in a potential employee. A prospective client that has to spend 20+ minutes on the phone to you explaining their business and what they do will not take another call from you as you have wasted their time. As a professional in the industry you need to exude a persona where clientele will come to you for your expertise and industry knowledge.

In order to get to know your client you should to do the following:

- Research their business. Google them, visit their website and other social media, even companies house where possible

- Visit one or more of their sites to see the business in operation where possible

- Speak to their employees to get an understanding of their business, their culture and the benefits of working for them, the staff turnover, their management style and the key decision makers within the organisation

Call and explore

Keeping in touch with clients is crucial. You really need to be the first person they think of when they have a new project. Apart from information gathering, there are hundreds of reasons to call your client; from asking about opening times, to share options or benefits, to an article you have seen in the press or who is running the restaurant for lunch. What you cannot find out about your client through research will have to be conducted through a phone call to them, or their employees directly. Your telephone calls will be made up of cold calls and warm calls.

A *cold call* is a telephone call made to someone who doesn't know you, what you are after or the reason for your call. They are often reluctant to talk to you. Not many people welcome sales calls, so cold calls should be planned out in advance with clear objectives. They should be friendly and non-hostile. Ideally you want the person at the other end of the phone to recognise your voice as someone friendly to talk to, and someone they want to engage with. Your cold call should be structured, and you should ask open-ended questions. Bear in mind that the person answering your call will try to end it if they feel intimidated, or that you are taking up too much of their time. Having only one or two objectives is ideal, this way you don't run the risk of tying up that person for too long, and potentially alienating them for future calls thus ruining your chances of gathering more information.

A *warm call* is a telephone call made to someone who either knows you, your company, or is expecting your call. Warm calls are easier to conduct as both parties already have a relationship and you can often get to the reason for your call immediately.

Some of the more important things you need to know about your client are:

1. An "organogram"

This is a company hierarchy or organisational chart detailing the people in head office and in charge of operations. This can be compiled through talking to candidates and the client, through social media and the Internet, or through networking.

2. Who are the decision makers?

Knowing who the ultimate decision makers are in any process is imperative to your success as a recruiter. A direct line and a strong relationship with them will greatly assist you in getting faster decisions and accurate feedback.

3. Key position holders

Knowing the heads of department and unit managers will also help in speeding up the recruitment process.

4. Rates they work to if they have a PSL (Preferred Supplier List)

This is really important: if the company already have a PSL in place then chances are you will be rejected upon first calling, and told to apply when it is up for renewal. This is a popular line many clients like to use to stop recruiters from phoning them all the time, so ensure that you ask for details about the PSL, when you can apply and to whom. You could also be wasting your time if it turns out that the client won't pay the rates you normally charge or adhere to your own payment terms. This is often the case with many large corporate clients. Understanding the potential revenue per placement for each client will be of great benefit to you in the long run.

5. Who else do they use - your competition

Map your competitors and understand the speed at which they work and the accounts they work on. If you know their recruitment methods you will easily be able to surpass their performance.

6. At what stage do they turn to agencies for help?

You need to know the recruitment activities your clients are undertaking and how long they have been recruiting each position, then adjust your search accordingly. The longer the client works on a job and the more activities they do, the less chance you have of placing the role, and the higher your fee should be.

7. What do you need to do in order to work with them?

Don't be afraid to ask this question outright of the client. They'll often give you an honest answer in return.

8. Their past experiences with recruiters

Almost every client will take the chance to talk to you about their bad experiences with recruiters. Use this information to formulate your recruitment strategy and pitch when the time comes. If you want to keep this client loyal to you, you mustn't make the same mistakes, and you should aim to create better experiences for them.

9. What do you expect from a recruitment company?

It is important to know your potential clients' expectations and ensure you live up to them and deliver every time you recruit for them. This will create loyalty and they will come to rely on you.

10. What do they look for in a candidate when recruiting?

Try and ask the decision makers this directly because it will help you in generating a shortlist of perfect candidates for them.

11. The annual recruitment spend?

Many corporate clients will have a recruitment budget and once depleted, they won't be able to use agencies. If you know their year-end date, then you'll know when to approach them and when not to.

12. When are they next recruiting and how often?

You need to understand each client's recruitment trends and staff turnover. This will help you categorise them and give you an understanding of their potential annual revenue so you can pre-plan your recruitment activities throughout the year. It can also indicate the urgency and speed you will need to operate.

13. Which roles are you currently recruiting throughout the organisation?

Don't forget to ask after all the roles they are recruiting because there may be some your colleagues can pick up. Be generous when passing leads across to your team.

What you really need to know in order to categorise each client is how much money they spend on recruitment each year, and what you need to do in order to get the "lions share" of it.

TIP: Spend the last half hour of your day planning your calls for tomorrow. Write down who you need to talk to and your objectives before you begin your day.

Decide on which companies to target based on your research and begin to form an industry-wide picture of which companies recruit the most and which agencies they use.

Remember that calling several contacts at one company on the same day will raise alarm bells and could get you blacklisted internally, particularly if you have to go through a receptionist or a switchboard every time. Spread out your calls to various clients and try and catch them when you know they will be at their desk and not busy in meetings.

TIP: Always be polite and try to smile when you are on the phone. It may sound silly, but you will eventually be able to tell when the person you're talking to is smiling or is uninterested.

Gatekeepers

Company secretaries and PA's are the gatekeepers you will most often encounter. They are the gateway to decision makers. They receive hundreds of calls a day and their job is to screen those worthy of being put through to the person you are after. By building rapport you can get on the good side of gatekeepers, but don't let them distract you from your daily tasks and objectives. Be nice to the point of getting something from them. Ultimately though, every gatekeeper needs to take a lunch break when the boss will be answering their phone themselves. The best time to call is during lunch break or after normal office hours. Be very prepared, or the day could come where you are put through to the contact you want and you don't know what to say and ruin the call through floundering. Not only will you look and sound like an amateur, but you will also ruin your standing with the gatekeeper after they get an earful for wasting their boss' time.

Punting for Business

A *canvass call* is a telephone call made to a client canvassing for business that you know exists, regardless of whether it is a warm or cold call. A *speculative call* is a telephone call canvassing for business that you may not exist, but where you are offering the client a product, (in our case the perfect candidate), for their business that they cannot refuse or pass up.

Through your business development activities you will know what your potential clients are looking for in a new employee. By thoroughly interviewing your candidates you'll know which client's they're suitable for. It is then up to you to call the client and speculatively sell your suitable candidate to the right contact or decision-maker.

Your sales pitch should be concise and well presented, selling the achievements, past experiences and skills of the candidate that the client is going to be most interested in. Each sales pitch will therefore be tailored to the client's wants.

Example of a speculative call:

"Hello Client, I have recently met with Candidate whom I think you will be very interested in. Candidate has recently been working for (x-business) running their Covent Garden site as the General Manager, financially responsible for taking £185k weekly in a 100-cover restaurant, leading a team 45 staff and 3 other managers.

Candidate previously worked for (y-business) for 5 years, 3 of which were as General Manager of their flagship site in Piccadilly Circus. Having started as a supervisor he progressed through to assistant manager and then to GM in less than 2 years!

Candidate is capable of running high volume sites of up to £200k weekly turnover, can lead and inspire teams of up to 100 staff and 5 managers and is fully financially responsible. When are you free to meet with him?"

The canvass call will differ slightly in that you can refer to the job that exists and directly match the candidate's skill set and achievements to the role's requirements.

Example of a canvass call: "I notice you are currently advertising for a General Manager in your (Leicester Square) site and I think Candidate would be ideal for the role."

In all instances, your objective should be to ensure that the client interviews your candidate and you should be committed to continue until you achieve that result from this client and any others you have planned to call that day.

In addition to planning your calls in advance, always have the candidate's notes and CV in front of you, their formatted CV ready to send when you do get an interview from the client, and make sure that you have covered the list of clients you are calling with your candidate and received their agreement.

Be sure you get all their current contact details, and details for the interview before you put the phone down. Also be sure to have your candidate's availability to hand. More often than not a client will not reschedule a speculative interview, particularly if they have given you a date and time where they can squeeze your candidate into their already busy schedule. Having to go back to the candidate and then to the client to rearrange will waste their time. Not only have you now lost the upper hand, but what guarantee is there that the client will answer your call a second time...?

Meeting your Clients

When getting to know your client it is always a good idea to meet them face-to-face, either outside of working hours or during the day at their place of work or head office. The benefits not only include being able to put a face to the name, but this will also provide you with insight on them as a person/interviewer that may be of use to your candidates. Being able to describe the interviewer or head office to a candidate through your own first-hand experience is invaluable.

Meeting with a client is a great way to take the next step in your business relationship. Ideally you should be meeting your current clients every 6-8 months to discuss the state of your business relationship and to see where any improvements can be made in your service to them and vice versa. Strengthening your client relationships will only increase the loyalty they have to you.

A client meeting is also a good way to get the answers to questions you have not yet covered during your business development activities. Client meetings can be either formal or informal. An initial client meeting should always be formal, organised and follow an agenda so you get the most out of the meeting. Informal meetings can follow an agenda, but will mostly be catch-ups with the client to discuss recent performances or any business needs they may have on the horizon for you.

There are 2 types of formal meetings:

A. To pitch for business

B. To pick up a new job

A. The Pitch for Business

There will be times when you are invited to pitch for business, either to be added to an existing PSL (preferred supplier list), or for the opportunity to work on a key role.

In all instances you can often be competing against other agencies.

A pitch for business should cover more than just yourself, you should also include your knowledge of the client to show them that you have done your research, and that your company or approach is somehow similar or in-line with theirs.

In a meeting such as this it is important to let the client know that you understand their business and their needs, but more importantly, that you are the best agency to use for this role, so it is very important to do as much research and preparation as possible for this meeting.

Often a presentation will be required for this form of meeting.

What your presentation should cover:

- Your company and an overview of what you do and the areas you cover

- Candidates and candidate attraction methods

- Highlight some of the clients you work with that are relevant to the client you are meeting. This allows them to feel confident that you have worked with a competitor and therefore understand their needs and the needs of this sector and that you have experience in this area

- Highlight some of the successful roles you have worked on

- Highlight how you work and how you propose to tackle this particular role or handle their account in general

- Highlight the key contacts in your business responsible for their account

- Finally; you should include your terms and your proposed terms of agreement with this client

Bearing in mind that this is a sales pitch; you need to highlight the main reasons that you are different to all the other agencies pitching for this same business throughout your presentation.

The more relevant your pitch is to their business, the more success in landing the account you will have.

B. To Pick up a New Job

A client meeting should always be arranged when picking up a new job in which you have no previous record with the client. If this has happened, then arrange a meeting and follow up with an email including a meeting agenda. This is so that you don't lose track of time and are able to get all the information you need to develop a fully comprehensive assignment brief.

1. Introductions

Firstly start with introductions and business card swapping. Take the time to appreciate the client's business card. It is polite. Thank the client for their time and introduce the agenda.

2. The Agenda

You should follow a structured approach much like a candidate interview. A meeting should not be longer than an hour. You should have a few pertinent questions ready for each section. This is information you need to build a company profile.

A basic meeting agenda will cover

- The person you are meeting, their background and their company

- The job role on offer and benefits

- The candidate requirements

- Fees and timescales

3. The Contact

Once seated, begin with a question or two about the person you are meeting with; how did they come to be in the role they are in, and what did they do before etc. This is your icebreaker. People often become more comfortable talking about themselves initially. It will also give you an idea of their knowledge and experience of the sector they're working in. Some managers are biased towards candidates with similar experience to themselves so bear this in mind when sourcing for them.

4. Their Company

Have a few relevant questions prepared to find out more about their recruitment needs such as annual staff turnover, the annual recruitment spend on agency, any new projects or key positions they will be or are currently recruiting for, any expansion plans and new openings planned. You want to get an idea of how much business this client will bring to your business, and into which tier or category they fall, as well as how many other agencies they tend to use and you'll be competing against. Then move onto their experience using recruitment agencies.

5. Their Experiences with Recruiters

It is this section you'll want to be taking a lot of notes, as these are going to be reflected in your sales pitch towards the end of your meeting. Ask direct questions; in their experience what it is that has not worked when using an agency? What do they want or expect from a recruiter? What can recruiters do better? How do they like to recruit? Who have they used and whom do they currently use? Why come to you? At what stage do they turn to an agency for help?

The answers to these questions will give you a good understanding of what they are looking for from you, and their expectations.

6. The Role on Offer

If you have arranged the meeting in order to pick up a new job then begin discussing the role here, filling in the information you failed to receive over the phone. This is covered in the previous chapter: The Job Cycle.

Areas you need to cover include:

- Job Title

- Salary

- Benefits and bonus potential

- Start date

- Duties and responsibilities

- Reporting structure

- Potential progression opportunities

- What are the most difficult aspects of the job

- Why the job became available

- What background would suit

- Culture fit and team

- What 3 things they would like to see on a CV for this role

Ask the client for some dates for interview now and get them to speculatively book it in their diary.

7. Your Business

By now you should have covered all the information you need to confirm your decision to work with this client and on the role if available. Now it is time to sell yourself and your company. If you have a company presentation to hand it is at this point where you can use it to introduce your company and your ways of working.

The idea behind this process is to get the client do all the talking prior to your sales pitch. The client will have highlighted what other recruiters have done wrong in the past and what their expectations are. Mirror your skill-set to their needs and tailor your company's unique selling points against the client's previous experience with recruiters in your closing statement.

For example:

If the client has said that previous recruiters would constantly send countless CV's to a job, of which only 2 or 3 CV's would match what the client was looking for. Previous recruiters would often take a week or longer to update the client on their efforts. The fees other agencies have charged have always been very high.

Your pitch would then go something like this:

"I believe that we can offer you exactly what you have been looking for in a recruitment partner. You said that previously you would receive countless CV's for one job and only 2 or 3 CV's would be relevant. We always strive to take a complete brief on every role so we only send you relevant CV's that match exactly what you are looking for. We don't believe in wasting your time with irrelevant CV's. We also don't believe in sending more than 4 CV's to job.

You said that previous recruiters would often take weeks to come back to you with updates; on every job we work on we will update you twice per week with where we are at with candidates and interviews so you don't have to worry about your assignment.

You stated that other recruitment companies have always charged high fees. We are happy to negotiate on our fees if you choose to go exclusive with us. In fact our retained assignments come with a significant saving off our standard fee...

We would be delighted to work with you (on this assignment/in an ongoing basis)."

TIP: *When the client is expressing their opinion on what other recruiters have been doing wrong, you should be taking notes and then choose the 3 most relevant ones for your closing statement.*

8. Fees & Negotiation

With enough practise pitching and a solid track record of success you'll eventually never have to negotiate on your fees. If you are starting out as a recruiter for a large company, chances are you won't have the opportunity to negotiate on fees unless you are accompanied by a line manager, or have their express permission beforehand. If your employer operates in this way then it is up to you to find out what the client is used to paying, and plan your pitch accordingly prior to your meeting with them. Find out how much room for negotiation you are allowed, and be prepared to stick to your guns.

Ensure you have a copy of your terms and conditions and your fees to give to the client, if you haven't sent them already, and be prepared to discuss any points that need clarification.

Ensure the client understands your payment terms and the conditions for a rebate, and then find out the contact details and address details where you will send your invoice for payment.

When pitching for business on a PSL it is often the client that dictates the fee level you will be working at and the payment terms. If you are pitching for business against other agencies for a project or a key role, the client may weigh up your fee and the benefits of using you against the other agencies they have met and against their budget and eventually come back to you to let you know your success. For one-off roles or with tier C clients, most often the fee is the deciding factor.

In all instances, weigh up the amount of work you will need to do in order to fill the job with the client, and the amount of jobs you will receive throughout the year from them, the timeframes in which the client needs the job completed, how long they've been looking, what they have already done and how many other agencies are working or have worked on the role. Thereafter consider your fee, and the fee the client is willing to pay. If it isn't worth it, then walk away.

In most cases a client will pay a higher fee for an urgent role if they believe that the benefits of using you outweigh the benefits of using another agency or doing the work themselves, or if they have tried and failed themselves.

If you have met with your client and explained to them what it is you do for your fee including all the stages involved in the process, they'll see the value you offer, and often won't feel the need to negotiate.

TIP: Never negotiate both your fees and your terms; it's one or the other.

9. Signing Terms

Never leave a meeting without having the client agree to your terms and getting them signed. If possible, have an iPad with your terms and get them to sign them on the spot. Paper terms will suffice.

After completing a successful placement your role doesn't end. Once offer and acceptance have taken place, there is often some time to go until the candidate starts in their new job. You still have to ensure the smooth transition of the candidate into their new role and ensure the client has followed up with the paperwork. Once the candidate has started you need to ensure that they successfully complete their probation period so you don't have to issue a credit.

Call the client every 2-3 weeks to check up on your starter, and ask if there is any other work you can help them with. This not only keeps you fresh in the mind of the client, but also shows you take an active interest in their business, your candidate and not just the pay cheque.

Many recruitment companies make the mistake of only working until they get paid. With so much competition for recruiters, you need to stand out from the rest to make a difference and add value to your client.

Strong relationships are the key to being a successful recruitment consultant. You should strive to maintain exclusive relationships with your key clients; where they come to you first before any other agency and are more than happy to deal exclusively with you on assignments.

Chapter 8: Food for Thought

Before you are let loose on the industry there are a few things you will need to take into account.

1. Buyers and Suppliers

At some point you will need to divide up your client base into 2 categories: buyers or suppliers. A *buyer* is a client who will "purchase" people from you. They will use your services and are willing to provide you with a number of jobs throughout the year. They are most often tier A or B clients. A *supplier* is a client who, for one reason or another, has decided not to work with you, or you may decide not to work with them. They then become your suppliers of staff; your headhunting grounds for supplying the rest of your client base.

You can't work with every client, but you can work with the best 2 or 3 clients in your sector. Always try and understand the competitors your clients favour, and if those competitors don't give you any business, then ensure they become a focused target for headhunting.

2. Control & Positioning

People are unpredictable; they will change their minds, their wants and their needs on a daily basis. If you are not in regular contact with your clients and candidates, checking their interest levels and testing their needs, you will be caught unawares. Once you lose control of a process with a client or a candidate, things can very easily spiral out of control.

The best way to make accurate forecasts of your business is to maintain control of your process and to position yourself as the first person both your clients and candidates turn to.

This becomes very easy when both parties trust you and see you are a source of knowledge and an expert in your field. Become a good listener, offer sound and honest advice and feedback, and build trustworthy relationships.

You must strive to maintain control of your processes at all times, for your own benefit, as much as for your clients and candidates.

3. The Competition

Much like mapping your industry with clients, it is a good idea to do the same with **your** competitors. Once you get to know who the other recruiters you compete against are, you will begin to form a picture of the accounts they work on or the clients they work with, which candidates they work with and how they source them, leading you to understand their recruitment methods and the speed at which they work.

With all this information at hand you will be able to easily work out which clients a candidate's details have been sent to, once they tell you which agencies they have registered with. You'll also be able to predict how active and successful the candidate has been in their job search.

4. Making a Difference and Standing Out

The basics of recruitment are the same across all industries, but the best recruiters are those that stand out and can make a difference. Whether that difference is with a simple "thank you" every day, going the extra mile for someone or being an industry leader and contributing to the community you will stand out for all the right reasons. Great recruiters bring their strengths and their own personalities to the role. Recruitment is a sales role, but it is a marketing role first and foremost.

Find the niche that you are most comfortable in, and find a group of clients who you can easily identify with and represent, who will turn to you before anyone else.

5. Candidate vs. Client; who is more important

Both are equally important and you cannot be successful without both. You should take every assignment seriously and ensure you complete it in a timely fashion. Represent your clients in the industry as if you are an ambassador of their brand, and always go the extra mile for them.

If you intend to make a career out of recruitment then know how to find those extra special candidates that everyone wants to hire and represent them exclusively throughout their career. Not only will this set you apart from every other recruiter in the industry, but your candidate will also eventually become a client and will have a long, positive history of dealing with you. Treat your candidates well and ensure you represent them with their best interests at heart. Help them achieve their career goals.

6. Proactive vs. Reactive Recruiting

Proactive recruiting is actively going out and finding great candidate for potential roles with clients, or *talent-banking* them and mapping the industry to build your candidate base. Reactive recruiting is responding to a recruitment need from a client once they have registered a role with you.

A good recruiter will seamlessly be able to operate with both methods; keeping an eye on the marketplace for great candidates and mentally *Talent Mapping* them for potential clients, and then arranging speculative introductions whilst conducting structured business development, picking up jobs and filling them.

Unless you are an Account Manager or internal recruiter, there is no excuse for sitting idle and waiting for the phone to ring.

7. Generating and Chasing Leads

Whether you are resourcing on job sites, or talking to clients and candidates, then you will inevitably hear about companies currently recruiting or their upcoming expansion plans. These are *leads* that can be followed up for more business, either by you or the relevant consultant whose remit it falls under. Work as a team to generate and pass leads to each other.

Chasing leads with clients should be treated as a speculative canvass call so you must always have one or two suitable candidates to hand showing the client you understand what they need. You should aim for a client meeting, or to book interviews if successful.

8. KPI's: The Formula

Key Performance Indicators (KPI's) are formulas based on your business activities and are used to measure the amount of work you do on a regular basis. Your company or your line manager will often be the ones to set your KPI's for you when starting as a trainee recruitment consultant.

Popular Key Performance Indicators include:

- BD Calls Made – Business Development Calls Made

- Client Visits - Client Visit Arranged or Attended

- Jobs Picked Up - The Number of Jobs Picked Up

- CVs Sent - The Total Number of CVs Sent

- Interviews Booked – The Total Number of Interviews Booked with Clients

- Candidate Calls – Number of Calls Made to Candidates

- Candidates Registered – Number of New Candidates Registered Face-to-Face

- Spec CV's – The Number of Speculative CVs Sent to Clients

- Placements – The Number of Placements Made

- Leads Picked Up – The Number of Leads Picked Up (and passed on)

When starting out as a recruiter you will need to spend a lot of time on the phone to cover your sector and to generate business by speaking to clients and candidates. KPI's are a good way to measure and focus your activities in the right areas.

KPI's are based on averages within the industry and are based on key activities you need to conduct in order to hit your company revenue targets. It is easier to explain them by working backwards.

Whilst it is true that you only need one candidate to make a placement, almost every client you will deal with will want to benchmark this candidate against two or even three other candidates at final stages. On average there are 3 interview stages performed by the client during the recruitment process. The client may want to see 4 or 5 candidates at first stage. Let's say you send 4 candidates and one gets placed. Your CV Sent to Placement ratio is 1:4. If you haven't understood the brief the first time round you may have to redo your initial shortlist and it will jump to 1:8

1:4 is a good ratio for a starting recruiter to aim for.

9. CV Sending and Volume

Find out exactly what your client expects from you in terms of CV volume. If they want you to send 10 or more CV's per job, chances are they don't know what they want or what they are looking for, and you could be wasting your time. Walk away from roles like this, unless the client agrees to go retained and pays you a portion of the fee upfront. Asking for money in advance is the best way to test their commitment.

Explain to your client why you prefer to send only 3 to 4 CVs per assignment, and offer to send them your longlist instead. This should satisfy anyone who requires proof of the amount of work you are doing.

When sending CV's, always attempt to send your shortlist in one go and include your candidate summary, and the reasons why each candidate is suitable for the role. Then follow your email up with a phone call to the client to discuss and book interviews.

10. Temp vs. Perm recruitment

This is a guide for Permanent Recruitment. Temp Recruitment is a numbers game and you will need to constantly be on the phone with candidates and clients drumming up business and filling weekly temp contracts. Many of your temps may even be waiting in the office from early on in the morning until you can find them work that day. Temp recruitment has a short candidate turnaround time and will push your skills and speed at which you work to the limit. Many temp recruiters that turn to permanent recruitment become successful very quickly.

Permanent recruitment is slower and more meticulous. You also need to take the candidates career into account and build relationships with both clients and candidates. If you are recruiting in the Perm arena you should be aiming for the long-term gains.

11. Growing your Success

So… what does it take to become a great recruiter and how do you measure your success? Truthfully. A lot. You've got 2 ears and one mouth… do the maths. Success is unique to each individual, but a successful recruiter should be aiming to improve his or her KPI ratio to 1:2. On average you should target 1 placement a week for high volume recruitment and 2 placements a month for retained assignments and senior placements. One board level placement per month can still earn you £30k+ in fees. Billing £10k monthly is the industry average for a recruitment consultant, with £12k being the benchmark for a senior consultant.

Be organised and plan in advance. Aim for long-term gains. Use daily planners and your diary to pre-plan your day and your week, blocking off enough time to get tasks done with a little bit of leeway should they overrun. Don't leave the office until tomorrow's objectives and activities have been planned. This way you can leave work knowing that tomorrow is already planned and enjoy your evening.

Work within your limits and work smart. Don't pick up jobs you know you can't fill or that you won't work on just for the sake of it. Taking on too much work may mean you miss out crucial steps in your job-filling methods or resort to shortcuts in an attempt to make up time.

Pick up the phone, get out-and-about, and network. You can't fill a job just using email.

Find the right clients for you then get to know them inside-and-out. Know what their ideal employee looks like and only send them candidates that match. Map the company and find out the key contacts and decision-makers so you always go to the right person immediately. Maintain your success and become the key recruiter for that account.

Be proactive and knowledgeable. Become trustworthy, reliable and a source of knowledge within the industry so people will be drawn to you. Be honest and offer free advice to those that need it.

12. Recruitment Standards and Ethics

As a recruiter, your reputation is everything. Regardless of which company you work for, your reputation is what will bring you success. How you treat clients and candidates, and the way in which you conduct yourself will all affect your reputation.

At all times it is imperative that you adhere to current legislation governing recruitment, particularly Data Protection. As an agency recruiter you must also abide by the law that governs being an agent e.g. you can only represent candidates that have given you their express permission to do so. The onus is on you to become familiar with all legislation governing the recruitment industry and to conduct yourself morally and ethically, and in accordance with legislation. Misrepresentation and a breach of legislation will reflect badly upon you before your company, and is often classified as gross misconduct as laid out in most company's handbook.

There are a number of professional bodies for recruiters and HR such as *The Institute of Recruiters* (www.theior.org.uk). Consider joining as a member, adhere to their codes of conduct, values and ethics and add value to our industry and upholding the professionalism in our industry.

Never forget - you are dealing with people's livelihoods and careers, so ensure you act in their best interests, and not to your own ends. Too many companies today are only focused on the profits they can make from peddling candidates to their clients that they neglect to teach you how to offer advice and guidance to job seekers. Seek to become knowledgeable, stay grounded and always try to add value.

Remember: *People buy from people*

About the Author

Stefan is an Anglicised Capetonian who has lived and worked in London since 2000 where he worked in Hospitality as a chef, bartender and then a manager for Oliver Peyton in the Michelin starred *ISOLA* before moving into the recruitment sector in 2003. Stefan started his recruitment with Hays and Randstad before holding the position of Regional Recruitment Manager for the largest Hospitality recruitment company in the UK. He was then a Partner in an Executive Search firm, launched an Executive recruitment arm for a London business before launching his own company in 2014. Stefan has been a company director since, specialising in internal recruitment and training recruiters for the IT and Hospitality sectors. He is an active member of the Institute of Recruiters, a member of Unite and an avid blogger, publishing articles about the recruitment industry, the economy in general in relation to recruitment, industry-related news for businesses and employees, and has reviewed restaurants and new openings around the UK.

Glossary

Hospitality industry – a broad collection of businesses within the service industry where guests and customers frequent, including restaurants, pubs and bars

Market Behaviour – the behaviours of customers or businesses in the industry

Culture – each company has a unique culture made up of their values and behaviours

Hierarchy – the management structure or ranks and divisions

Spaghetti flinging – a term used to describe a volume-based recruitment business model where a large number of CV's are submitted per job in the hopes that one or two will eventually be taken to interview stage. Much like throwing spaghetti at a wall; some will eventually stick.

Database – a company database is found on a computer and houses all company information on clients, candidates and jobs

Search parameters – specific requirements of a job or candidate that are used to construct a search on a database

Brief – a job description and candidate description given by a client describing what they are looking for

Long list – a list of all the applicants for a specific job that you have considered, including any found in searches and headhunting exercises you have done

360-degree recruitment – the ability to recruit all 3 cycles; clients, candidates and jobs

Agencies – a recruitment company

3rd party databases – refers to online job boards or websites where candidates can uploads their CV's so employers and agencies can find them

LinkedIn – a social media networking website

Account Management – the management of corporate accounts, often large, branded businesses that submit new vacancies every week, only requiring matching candidates to be submitted. An account manager will often only need master the candidate cycle and will work on a handful of accounts at any one time.

Corporate Accounts – large, multi-unit businesses. Corporate companies and large branded or chain businesses

Live vacancies – jobs that you are currently working on that have not yet been filled

Headhunting – the act of searching, finding and approaching candidates based on specific parameters or companies for clients in order to fill jobs

Talent Map – A strategic tool used in proactive headhunting. The act of creating a list or a map or prospective candidates for specific clients or companies and mapping them out for future reference

Job hoppers – someone who changes jobs frequently; can vary from every year or every 6 months.

Return on Investment (ROI) – the benefit received after investing an amount of time or money

Books – refers to the candidates you are either actively representing or have registered on your company database

Right to Work in UK – a legal requirement requiring specific documents for anyone looking to be employed in the UK as a full-time worker

Laws on Compliance – government regulatory practices, laws and policies

Standard practises – the accepted business practises that all industry businesses should follow

Coversheet – a brief introductory paragraph accompanying a CV, explaining to the client the reasons the candidate has been submitted for the vacancy

 Notice Period – the legally required number of week's work a candidate has to complete once they have resigned from their job. The time period between the receipt of a letter of termination of employment and their last working day.

UK Data Protection Act – a UK law governing the storage and usage of personal data

Closed question – a question with a YES or NO answer

Open question – a question often requiring the interviewee to talk at length and can includes the words: How, When, Why and What

PSL – a Preferred Supplier List and Agreement where a client has a list of authorised suppliers they are allowed to use for recruitment in this instance

Speculative sale – the act of phoning a client and discussing a candidate you have met with explaining why they are a perfect fit for the client's business regardless of there being a live vacancy or not

Terms of Business – a legal document outlining the terms on which you trade with your clients

Terms and Conditions – see Terms of Business

Service Charge – an often-optional charge listed on a bill in a restaurant for the service the staff have provided

TRONC – the weekly service charge generated from trade and held by the business. Applies to the restaurant industry.

Headers – the job title or subject line used when advertising a job

Hooks – the attractive benefits of a job used to entice candidates to apply for your job

Catchment area – a geographical area or radius relating your job search that is reasonable distance for candidates

Unique selling points – the unique features of your recruitment business in relation to every other recruitment business

Reputation – the industry wide opinion of your business practices and code of conduct

Bedding in – a time period in which you or your candidate is getting to know their job

Guarantee Period – also known as a rebate period, this is a length of time your terms of business state that you will provide the client with remuneration in the event the candidate is unsuccessful

New desk – in recruitment; recruiting a set of vacancies with a set of clients that has not been attempted before in a particular company

Existing desk – a collection of clients and vacancies already being operated on by a specialised recruitment consultant, or one that has been recently vacated, in a specific sector

Business development – the act of building relationships with clients with the goal of finding and filling jobs

Relationship building activities – any activity which may enhance your already existing relationship with a client

Warm contacts – a client contact that is familiar with either you or your company

Cold contacts – a client contact that is unaware of you or your business

Warm calls – a call made to a contact that is either familiar with you, happy to speak with you, or is expecting your call

Cold calls – a call made to a cold contact that is also unaware of the reason for your call

Open-ended questions – see open questions

Gatekeepers – company secretaries, switchboard operators or PA's that you have to get past in order to speak to your target contact

Punting for business – the act of business development and asking for jobs to work on

Canvass call – a call made canvassing for business that you know exists

Speculative calls – a call made canvassing for business where none that you know of exists

Mapping your industry – creating a list of existing competitors and businesses currently trading in your industry

 Proactive recruiting – recruitment activities done before a need arises, such as Talent mapping

Reactive recruiting – waiting for a recruitment need to arise and then conducting recruitment activities

Talent banking – see talent map

Leads – an opportunity for business or to pick up a job

Key performance indicators – numbers used to measure your productivity during a certain time period; daily, weekly and monthly

About this guide

This guide is for anyone thinking of starting a career in recruitment, for anyone who wants to know about the job of a recruitment consultant and what it entails, for anyone who has just started in the industry and wants to build on the training they have received.

This guide provides a good overview of the role of a recruitment consultant and what the job entails. It goes into detail about all aspects involved with the recruitment process, from starting on a new desk, to dealing with candidates, clients and the job life cycle. You will learn a whole range of skills ranging from how to search for, and interview candidates, how to find suitable clients and win business from them, to picking up jobs and filling them. This guide will provide you with all the information and basics you need to survive your first year in recruitment and beyond.

www.ingramcontent.com/pod-product-compliance
Lightning Source LLC
Chambersburg PA
CBHW071236170526
45165CB00003B/1122